Clay Creatures

Laura Vogelnest

Contents

Rigby

A Harcourt Achieve Imprint

www.Rigby.com
1-800-531-5015

Introduction

Before you make clay creatures, you will need to know how to:

make a ball,

make a pancake,

make a rope.

You will also need:

a craft stick,   a pencil,

some clay.

Make a Ball

Roll the clay around and around
between your hands to make a ball.

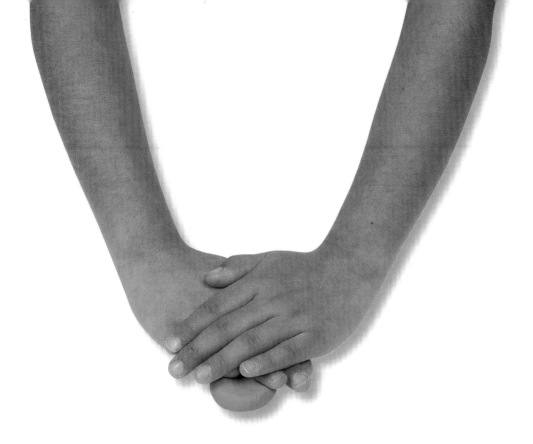

Make a Pancake

First, make a ball. Then press
the ball down. Make it flat like
a pancake. Smooth out any cracks.

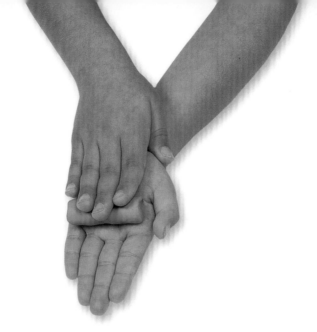

Make a Rope

Roll the clay back and forth between your hands to make a rope.

Roll it more for a thinner, longer rope.

Roll it less for a thicker, shorter rope.

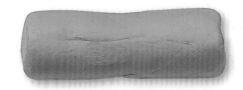

Make a Caterpillar

Roll lots of balls. Then press the
balls together.

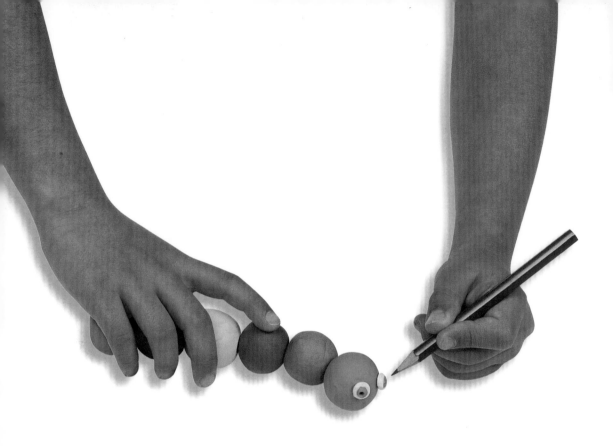

Roll four tiny balls. Press them on well. Then use the pencil to finish the eyes.

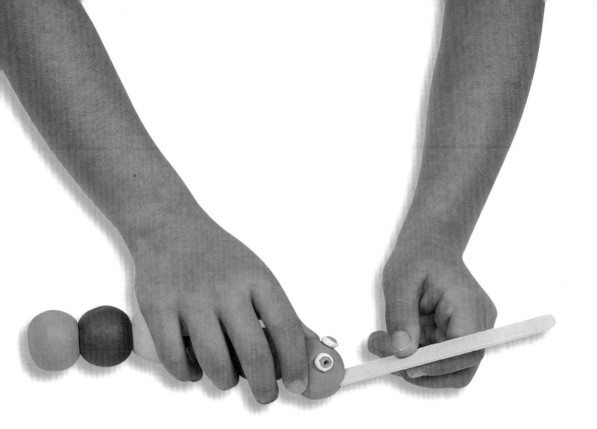

Use the craft stick to make the mouth.

Roll short ropes for the feelers and the legs. Press them on well.

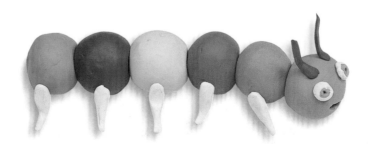

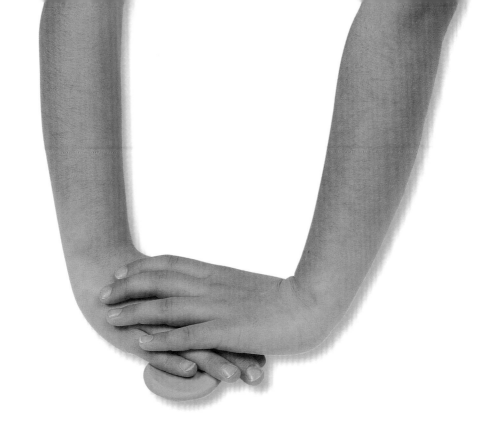

Make a Turtle

Make a pancake for the turtle's shell.
Then roll four short ropes for the legs.

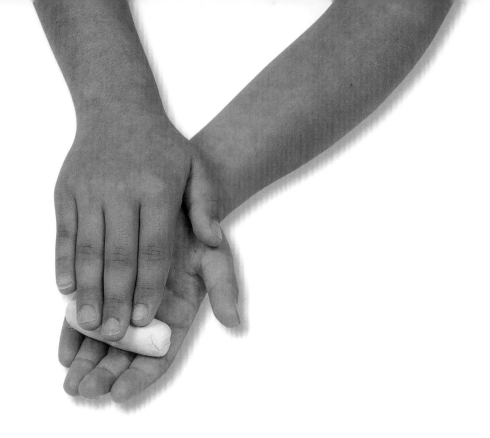

Roll a longer, thick rope for the turtle's head. Then roll a shorter, thin rope for the tail.

Press the six ropes under the
shell. Press them on well.

Roll two tiny balls. Press them on
well. Then use the pencil to finish
the eyes.

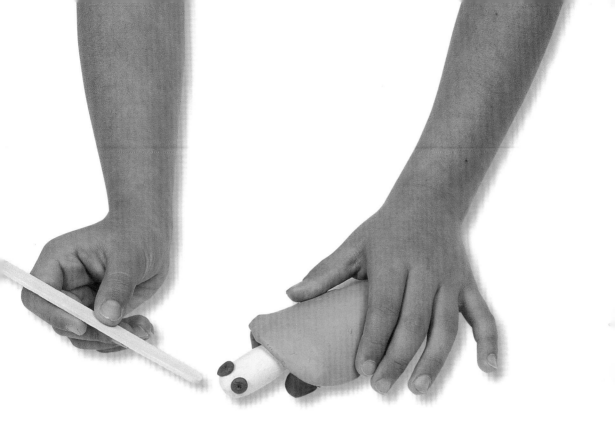

Use the craft stick to make the mouth.

What other creatures can you make?